Secrets of the Silence

the power of praying without words

a 21 day journey of prayer

Bob Kilpatrick

Secrets of the Silence

the power of praying without words

a PrayerCanvas book

©2009 Bob Kilpatrick
All rights reserved. This book is protected by the copyright laws of the United States of America. Copying any portion of this book without prior written permission, except for review or the use of short quotations, is expressly forbidden.

Additional copies of this book and other
PrayerCanvas materials
are available by visiting

prayercanvas.com

bobkilpatrick.com

or write to;

PrayerCanvas
Bob Kilpatrick Ministries, Inc.
P.O. Box 2383
Fair Oaks, CA 95628
(discounts given on multiple copies)

For Cindy

"The notes are silver,
The rests are gold!"
-Mozart

Introduction

We generally think of prayer as something we speak out loud. We ask the blessing on our food, bring our prayer lists to God and go through them line by line; our pastor opens the worship service with prayer, prays for the offerings and sends us off with a benediction.

Prayer is for most of us an SOS raised toward heaven in times of trouble. There is nothing wrong with that at all. God wants to and will be our help! Even for those of us who pray every day, through good and bad times, our prayers are mostly requests- "God, do something here. Act on our behalf."

But there is a secret; when we come before Him in silence, God answers even the prayers we never pray. God listens to our hearts. Even more encouraging, He already knows our needs and is more than willing to guide us and provide for us.

There is power in speaking aloud our concerns and delights to God. There is an equal, and perhaps even greater, power to silence in prayer. Isaiah said "In quietness and confidence shall be your strength." (30:15) It is into this strengthening quietness that I want to lead you as we go through this book.

I have heard it said that it takes three weeks to make a new habit or break an old one. Over the next twenty one days as you read this book you can make a new habit of prayer that will strengthen you and give you confidence and greater joy in God's presence.

I want to invite you on a three week journey of silent prayer and stillness before the God of Love. Our ultimate intention is not to replace your spoken prayers but to enhance them with a power that only comes in the secret place with God, in quietness and stillness.

The book is in three sections, each with seven chapters. I encourage you to read a chapter each day for three weeks. Set aside a special time each day to read and pray. Early morning is a good time for a variety of reasons:
- it is your first activity of the day,
- there are fewer disturbances, and
- it will help set the tone for the rest of your day.

Regularity of practice is the enemy of complacency. If your schedule will not permit the same time, make sure that you set aside a time each day in advance. Prearranging your prayer time will help you keep to it.

Set aside a special place where you can be undisturbed for the entire time you spend with God. If that is not practical, choose a kind of place- a bedroom, a garage, a hotel room, the car, an empty office, on a walk- where you know you can be alone. As we form this habit of a regular meeting place, we will come to expect to meet God in the silence when we enter.

Limit your visual and aural stimulation as much as possible. Perhaps this is why King David calls it the "secret place" and Jesus talks about the "closet of prayer" in the Bible. Turn off the television and the radio, close your computer, refrain from speaking... be still.

Decide on a length of time that you will spend in the silence each day and stick with it. Don't be idealistic and over reach your attention span. Ten, twenty, thirty minutes are all good. Do what you can. Again, prearrange this and stick to it. If you use a planner, enter the time of day and length of time you'll spend in silence just like you would any other appointment.

Create an environment that is suitable for prayer. Listen to the PrayerCanvas ambient prayer music that was produced specifically for this purpose. You might close the door, pull the curtains, dim the lights- whatever will minimize your distractions.

Let everyone in your household or workplace know of your commitment and ask for their respect of it. Make it a sacred meeting, one not to be disturbed, not even by the seemingly urgent needs of the day. If you still find yourself constantly interrupted, find another more suitable time and place to practice silence.

Do not combine your time with God with other responsibilities, such as making chore lists or planning your day. You are called to this time for one purpose only- to meet God in the silence. Keep it sacred and inviolable.

However, if you find yourself distracted by thoughts of responsibilities, keep a note pad nearby so that you can jot these thoughts down and dismiss them immediately from your mind. As soon as possible you should learn to do without the note pad and discipline yourself to reject these thoughts.

Resist the urge to simply make this a reading time. The Bible or Christian books are good, but are they better than Jesus Christ Himself? We come to this time for one purpose; to meet God in person and learn to hear His voice. Don't let even good things keep you from the best thing.

I also want to invite you to take an unusual challenge;

-Make a prayer list before you begin. Use the page at the back of the book titled <u>My Prayer List</u>. Write down all the concerns you would be speaking to God in your prayer times.

- Be specific. The more general your prayers are (i.e., "for peace in the world" or "that You should bless our family") the less likely you are to be able to identify actual answers to prayer. Specific prayers get specific answers.

- Make it as complete a list as you can. "in *everything*… let you requests be known to God." (Phil 4:6)

- Set it aside for the next three weeks. You won't be referring to it at all during this time. We'll come back to it at the end of the book to see whether God has been at work on your behalf while you have been with Him in silence.

Each day we will consider a Scripture and an aspect to silent prayer. You'll learn the secrets and experience the power that God has promised to those who seek Him. These secrets are not occult practices unknown to the masses. They are not unknown, they are simply not done.

After teaching His disciples the night before the crucifixion, Jesus told them "now that you know these things, you will be blessed *if you do them*." (John 13:17, italics added) The secret is that this kind of prayer actually works, but the power is only experienced in the doing.

"He who dwells in the secret place of the Most High shall abide under the shadow of the Almighty." (Psalm 91:1)

Let's go to the secret place to find the secrets of the Silence.

Week One

The Power of Silence

1.1

Silence Is…

"Surely I have calmed and quieted my soul." Ps. 131:2

Listening to God is more important than anything else you will ever do. Ever, in all your days. It is more important than your prayer requests, worship, Bible reading, fellowship, witnessing, preaching or any work you do on God's behalf. There is nothing, no matter how saintly or necessary it may be or appear, that is more essential to your life.

John tells us "In the beginning was the Word, and the Word was with God and the Word was God." (John 1:1) God is expressive. He desires to communicate with us. He is a person and He is seeking a relationship with you. If you believe that "the word of God is living and powerful," (Heb. 4:12) it is then imperative that you hear Him.

Listen.

Silence is the medium. It is necessary to cease our activities, eliminate our distractions, close our mouths and open our ears to the voice of God. He has promised to speak to us if we will listen.

The silence we seek in prayer and meditation is not simply to stop speaking but to quiet our hearts. It is not an outward rule to follow but a state of being to have. We can self-impose a strict 'no talking' rule without ever having stilled our spirits in the way that makes us most receptive to God's Spirit.

Still.

Quiet.

Rest.

When Elijah heard the voice of God outside the cave in 1 Kings 19 the King James Bible called it a "still, small voice" while another translation called it "the sound of gentle stillness" and still another described it as a "delicate whispering voice." These are picturesque, and they also show us that God is wanting us to be still enough to hear the delicate whispering of His voice that the din of our lives can so easily drown out.

Why is silence and stillness so important? Can't God speak to us in every circumstance? Surely He can and does speak to us whenever we are listening. It is the listening that is so difficult to do in the midst of activity, noise and other distractions.

If you want to hear from God you must listen for His voice. Rarely does God overpower us with His speaking. As with Elijah, He isn't in the thunder, the whirlwind or the earthquake. He speaks softly. So we still our hearts to hear Him.

We cannot have a quiet heart simply by closing our mouths. That's a good start but not a good finish. As we close our mouths we must also open our ears and hearts to the Holy Spirit. We surrender all of ourselves to His scrutiny. We wait patiently before Him as a servant does to his master or a student does to his teacher. We listen for the delicate, whispering voice of God.

Here is the first secret of the silence; it is for listening. You cannot listen well while you are speaking. To truly hear we must quiet our voices, minds and spirits. In any conversation one must be silent while another speaks.

Do you believe that God wants to speak to you?

We can know about God by reading the Bible. He will sometimes make some particular scripture come alive to us- we say He speaks to us- as we read it. However, God is more than the sum of the words on the pages of the Holy Bible. He is a person and He desires to be known.

As one hymn writer said "Beyond the sacred page, I seek Thee, Lord." God wants to be known and knowing Him comes by hearing Him. As we listen, God reveals Himself to us. This is the amazing truth of Christianity; God will reveal Himself to anyone who will seek Him out.

"Father, give me a quiet and listening heart today. I come to listen and to know You. Thank You for calling me Your own and revealing Yourself to me."

1.2

The Peace of Silence

"O, Death, where is your sting? O, Grave, where is your victory?" 1 Cor. 15:55

There are two kinds of power to silence. The first kind, which we will discuss today, happens within us. It is exemplified most in the confidence we have before God and in ourselves. This power of silence is the power of surrender.

There is a peace that comes from surrender. In that act we offer everything to God and have nothing else to lose. No one can take from us what we have already freely given. If we have surrendered our very lives, what is the worst that can happen to us? Death? Even that has no power over us when we surrender to God.

"I will ransom them from the power of the grave;
I will redeem them from death.

O Death, I will be your plagues!
O Grave, I will be your destruction!"
Hosea 13:14

In the quietness of our own souls we are no longer afraid. When we are truly still before God there is nothing that can disturb the peace we have. Dorothy L. Sayers used a phrase in one of her books, "the still center of the spinning world." This is very like where we meet and abide with God.

The world may be in chaos, our circumstances may be trying, yet when we come before the Lord of heaven and earth and quiet our hearts before Him, we hear Him speak as the Prince of Peace.

Peace.

Be still.

Philippians 4 says that we are to be anxious for nothing and to pray about everything. As we do, Paul says, the peace of God which is beyond our understanding will guard our hearts and minds in Christ Jesus. It is this incomprehensible peace that we experience in the silence.

We no longer fear God. We have been exposed before Him and lived. We have been accepted in the Beloved. He has purified us without destroying us. He has taken us through death into the power of the resurrection.

We learn in our silence before Him that God, who is all powerful, is also infinitely good. We can trust Him with our deepest fears and our most trifling concerns. He who counts the hairs on our heads will care for the smallest and greatest needs we have.

We no longer fear man. If we have come through a face to face meeting with God there is surely nothing any man can do to us that would strike fear in us. Personal attacks, persecution, hardships and suffering all lose their power over us in the silence.

We are confident before God. He knows us, has forgiven us and made us new. There is no accusation against us that the cause of which has not been already exposed within us and given up to God. Though the wicked flee even when no one pursues, we stand confident and fearless.

Our confidence, however, is not in anything of ourselves- our abilities, good deeds or righteousness. We have laid all that at the feet of Jesus. Our confidence is in Christ alone. Paul tells us plainly in 2 Cor. 12:9-10 that he gloried in his weakness because in it God was strong.

Isaiah 30:15 says "In returning and rest you shall be saved; in quietness and confidence shall be your strength." Hebrews 4:9 says "There remains therefore a rest for the people of God." Silence is the sound of rest and restoration. Stillness is the first sign of inner confidence and strength.

"Dear Father, give me a quiet heart that I might hear You, know You and walk with You. Let the peace and confidence of Your life be evident in me today."

1.3

The Second Power of Silence

"Be silent, all flesh, before the Lord ; for he is aroused from his holy habitation." Zech. 2:13

The second kind of power in silence happens outside of us. God is roused from His silence on our behalf. He speaks up for those who have no voice. He protects those who trust in Him. He shows Himself strong for the weak.

David said in Psalm 3:3 "You, O Lord are a shield for me." He is our strong tower. We hide ourselves in God and allow Him to be our protection. But God will not act on our behalf if we have taken that responsibility on our own shoulders. We will not be safe in His strong tower if we do not run into it. He lets us fight our battles if we will.

Our silence and stillness indicates that we are not trusting ourselves but God. We are still while He is active; quiet while He speaks up for us. When we are weak He is strong. We are not the defender but the defended; not the protector but the protected; not the provider but the provided for.

We can spend so much time and energy defending our status, position, possessions, relationships and rights. When we are with Jesus in the silence we cede these to Him. Since all we are and have are His, He may do with us as He will. We can rest knowing He gives all good things to those He loves.

When we are still and quiet before God we allow Him the freedom to do what He wants to do in us, through us and for us. We forego so many blessings because we take on our own shoulders what God means to carry for us. In the silence we learn to abandon ourselves to Him and trust Him completely; to lay our burdens on His shoulders.

During a particularly trying summer I was earnestly praying every morning for one or two hours about a pressing need that was weighing on my mind. This went on for two months. Each morning I sat with my open Bible on my knees and prayed.

Over the course of the months I noticed that I spoke my prayers aloud less and less. The last few weeks the most I said was simply "You know." I told no one about the need. I simply sat in His presence and meditated on Him, listening for His voice and finding my rest in the silence.

One morning I received a call from a friend. He told me that he had been praying for me for weeks and knew he had been called by God to help me in some way. He asked specifically what I was praying about. I told him about the need I was lifting up to God. Over the two months I was praying God had spoken to him to meet this need, which he did that day.

Moses told the Israelites in Exodus 14: 13-14 to "stand still and see the salvation of the Lord, which He will accomplish for you today.... The Lord will fight for you, and you shall hold your peace."

The Hebrew meaning for "hold your peace" in this verse is "be quiet." In their stillness and silence God won the victory for His people.

Do you believe that God loves you and calls you His own?

What have you taken on your shoulders

that God is calling you to put on His?

What battle are you fighting that God would fight for you if you let Him?

What needs are you holding instead of giving them up to the lover of your soul?

> *"The name of the Lord is a strong tower;*
> *The righteous run to it and are safe."*
> Prov. 18:10
>
> *"Cast your burden on the Lord,*
> *And he will sustain you;*
> *He shall never permit the righteous to be moved."* Ps. 55:22
>
> *"... casting all your care upon Him*
> *for He cares for you."* 1 Peter 5:7

"Dear Father, give me a confidence in your love and power today. Help me to lay all I am and have on You."

1.4

The Purpose of Silence

"Now the Lord came and stood and called as at other times, 'Samuel! Samuel!' And Samuel answered, 'Speak, for Your servant hears.'" 1 Sam. 3:10

Silence is listening. As we saw in Psalm 81, God desires that we first listen to Him, then walk in His ways. When we come to the silence we are adopting a receptive attitude, a humble and open heart and a willing spirit.

It takes time for us to feel comfortable with silence. We are so accustomed to filling the air with noise. But here there are no radio, television, computer or other distractions. We have come to do one thing; sit quietly and listen to God.

Meditate.

We may have been raised to think that meditation is too mystical and can lead to deception. We can shy away from it because the word has been co-opted. We should never let this kind of fear keep us from the pursuit of God.

First, let us be very clear; Christianity is mystical. We believe in a God we cannot see who desires to communicate with us. We believe in an invisible spiritual dimension to the universe that is teeming with life and full of activity. We were created to be a part of it.

Second, Jesus made a promise to us that if we asked God for a good gift He would not allow us to receive anything harmful. In Matthew 7 He says if we, being evil, know how to give good gifts to our children, "how much more will your Father who is in heaven give good things to those who ask Him!"

If we are seeking God we are fully and completely protected from the enemy of our souls. God will give us good things as we seek Him. Not only does He allow this, He encourages it.

In fact, He is calling you to it.

"When I remember You on my bed

I meditate on You in the night watches."
Ps. 63:6

*"Let the words of my mouth
and the meditations of my heart
be acceptable in Your sight, O Lord,
my strength and my redeemer."*
Ps. 19:14

*"I meditate on all Your works;
I muse on the work of Your hands."*
Ps; 143:5

Meditation requires silence so that we may listen with our hearts. We step away from the stimulations of the outward world and remove ourselves to the inner, spiritual place- the secret place- with God. We do not do this without counsel.

Our counsel is in the Scriptures. In Psalm 1 David says that the blessed man meditates "in His law" day and night. It can be helpful to begin your prayer time by reading the Bible. You might even leave it open to be a 'second voice' or an 'amen' to you as you commune with the Spirit of God.

It can also be helpful to remember the works of God- to muse on the works of His hands.

We can ponder the majesty of nature, the grandeur of His salvation, the beauty of scripture or His faithfulness and kindness to us. This serves to open our hearts and ears to Him. But we cannot stop at merely thinking about God.

The purpose of the silence is to listen for the voice of God, learn to recognize it and to understand what He is saying to us. The silence is like a blank canvas on which He paints, an instrument on which He plays or an empty stage on which He speaks.

We are not the performers, we are the audience. We attend to God and wait on Him. It is not our time to speak or act. In this moment, in this place, words and activity are a distraction. We behold Him, face to face.

He speaks.

We listen.

"Father, I will meditate on Your law and works today and remember Your loving-kindness to me. Speak to me as I sit with You."

1.5

The Posture of Silence

"So Jacob called the place Peniel: 'For I have seen God face to face, and my life is preserved.'" Gen. 32:30

This word- Peniel - is used in the Old Testament to describe the relationship God desires to have with us. It means to be "face to face with God." We may imagine ourselves at some middle distance from God looking His way, but the phrase has a specific dimensional meaning.

It means to be knee to knee, hip to hip, shoulder to shoulder, chin to chin, eye to eye, breath to breath- so close that there is no distance between us. In ancient times this was called the kiss of worship.

The Maori men of New Zealand greet each other by holding their faces so close as to touch noses and exchange breath. This is a perfect picture of what Peniel is and what God wants for us.

And it certainly gives fuller meaning to the Holy Spirit being called the Pneuma- the breath of God. God desires to whisper to us as we are Peniel, face to face with Him. He wants to speak to us and breathe into us at the same moment.

As He whispers to us His word carries life and breath for us. There is no other way to receive His breath than to be Peniel- breath to breath, face to face with Him. It is in the silence that we receive the breath of God.

Previously I told you about two months of earnest praying I did that ultimately led me to meditative silence in God's presence. The seeds of this book were sown in that experience.

I learned a new way to pray that I call Pneuma praying. I was breathing out my prayers and breathing in His life. Since He knows my needs before I ask, there is nothing to be said in that moment. I merely receive Him.

Inspire- to breathe in.

It is the exchange of spirit and life in the

silence that gives you strength and grace to face the circumstances of the life to which God has called you. Isaiah says they that wait on the Lord will renew their strength and will mount up like eagles. (Is. 40:31) Waiting comes before mounting up; listening comes before walking (Ps. 81:13). God will always call us away to the secret place before He sends us out. Our renewal happens in the stillness, waiting on God, Peniel.

The purpose of the silence is that you might hear God, understand your place in Him, be filled with His strength and go out with confidence to live for Him. We cannot hurry the waiting. Like sleep it is a time for restoration, rebuilding and strengthening.

In too many lives the silence of private prayer is bypassed in favor of the communal gathering of the Church or other public worship experiences. God does not call us first to the Church but to Himself. We are His alone, set apart. Only after that are we given to each other. The most important service of worship we have is to sit at His feet alone and learn of Him.

Corporate worship is a vital part of the life of the Christian community, but it can never replace the Peniel God desires for us. We are each called to be with God, closing the door on the rest of the world and seeking Him alone. The wonderful benefits of corporate worship are sweeter for this solitary quiet time.

What will make us strong to run without growing weary is the unhurried, solitary time of waiting on God. All our fellowship with other Christians is a far second in importance to our fellowship with Him.

Do not mistake activity for fruitfulness or maturity. Do not think that all you need from God can be had in the gatherings with other Christians. There are some things- the most important things- that you can only get one on one, face to face, breath to breath, alone with God.

"Lord Jesus, breathe Your Spirit into me as I come close to You, closing the door to the world outside, closing the distance between us. Let your life and strength be mine. Amen."

1.6

The Practice of Silence

"But the Lord is in His holy temple. Let all the earth keep silence before Him." Hab. 2:20

To quiet one's heart in the presence of God can be frightening. Perhaps we are carrying guilt from activities we know are wrong. Perhaps we are ashamed or feel unworthy. We may not be ready to surrender our lives to God's will. These will all keep us from the stillness.

I took my first writing retreat a few months after my father passed away in 1991. I got alone in a cabin on a mountain side- no television, radio, computer or telephone. I was alone with God for a week. It was very uncomfortable. The first day it seemed as though all my worst traits came to my mind when I silenced my heart.

I felt all those emotions I mentioned- shame, guilt, fear, unworthiness- and I had six more days to be here. I didn't know if I could do it. As I persevered, though, it grew easier and more comfortable. I confessed my failings and accepted God's forgiveness.

I said like David in Psalm 69, "O God, You know my foolishness and my sins are not hidden from you." I had avoided this meeting because I didn't want to talk with God about my life. Yet that is the way to life and freedom. If you are unwilling to be still and listen, this book will be of no use to you.

The silence we want is unguarded before God. We are uncovered in His presence. There is no hiding, no disguise. We are alone before Him. There is no other to take His gaze away from us. We are searched and known by Him.

This is a terrifying thing to experience- to be known in all our weakness and sin- yet this is the road to freedom. Once we surrender ourselves to it and abandon ourselves to God we find that the fire He brings to us is not to destroy us but to purify us.

Begin your prayer time with a confession- "Lord, all of my life is open before You. Every act and attitude is known to You. I cannot hide myself nor can I change myself. I put myself in Your loving hands."

This is where we must begin; in surrender and abandonment. In our silence we are open, humbled, guileless and unprotected before our Creator. He does not call us to change ourselves but to offer ourselves to Him. Romans 12:1- "I beseech you therefore, brethren, that you present your bodies a living sacrifice."

We do not sacrifice ourselves. Rather, we present our bodies to God and let Him do as He will. Once again, we find that surrender and abandonment are our starting points. We cannot start from any other posture. We cannot be a friend of God until we have become the subject of God, conquered and ruled by Him alone.

In our silence before God we offer no defense of our lives, no explanation of our actions, no deflecting of responsibility, no judgment of ourselves whatsoever. We accept His opinion and assessment of us alone. We wait before Him and listen.

This is another secret of the silence. It is not an act of refusing to talk, as a petulant child might do, or of withholding information. God knows all. Silence is the posture of humility and receptivity. In this silence before God we come to know that He knows all, loves all and will deal kindly with us.

In Luke 9 when Peter spoke up on the Mount of Transfiguration, God overshadowed him and said "this is my beloved Son; hear Him." Peter had, as many of us do, a habit of speaking when words are unnecessary. It is an act of discipline to remain silent and receptive. What God told Peter He also tells us- "hear Him."

It is also an act of trust to remain silent before God. He knows our needs before we tell them to Him. He loves us with an everlasting love. If we believe these things, we can rest knowing that our God not only knows our needs but will care for us.

Quiet your heart. Do not defend, explain, dismiss, deflect, argue or suggest. Adopt a posture of complete openness to God. Raise no weapon. Guard no battlement. Do not shield your heart. Lay it all down. Lay yourself down. Present yourself as a living sacrifice.

"Loving God, I am Yours. Everything I am and everything I have I lay before You. I abandon myself to You completely. Speak to me Your words of life."

1.7

The Character of Silence

"There remains therefore a rest for the people of God." Heb. 4:9

In chapter one we referred to Elijah hearing the voice of God outside the cave in 1 Kings 19.

The still, small voice.

The sound of gentle stillness.

The delicate whispering voice.

God calls to us in the sound of gentle stillness because that is who He is. It is essential to His nature. Though active, He is forever at rest. Though moving, He is forever still. Though speaking, He is forever silent- the sound of gentle stillness. God is in the silence. He is the silence.

God is the still center of the spinning world.

God calls us to have His nature; to be like Him in every particular way. It is no surprise, then, that He would want us to have the same essential stillness that He enjoys. In fact, He woos us to the secret place, the cleft of the rock, the closet of prayer so that we can experience the silence and stillness with Him and learn to live perpetually in that state as He does.

We take on the characteristics of those to whom we listen and with whom we spend time. Children act like their parents, disciples act like their teachers. God calls us to Himself so that we may be like Him. His ultimate purpose is that you should be "conformed to the image of His son, Jesus Christ." (Rom. 8:29) He has called you to bear the familial likeness.

Here is another secret of the silence; in it you are conformed to God's image. You take on His character by being with Him, opening your heart to Him. You may try every way to bend yourself by your own strength into the image and character of Christ but it will not work.

You may read all His commands and be faithful to do them but the essential likeness and life of God is missing. It is only gained in the abandonment of yourself to Him and His mercy, the surrender of your soul, the quietness of your heart. It can only be had by time spent with Him alone.

Paul wonderfully opens this truth to us in Galatians. He asks in chapter three if we are able to finish in our own power what God has started in us by His Spirit. The answer is, of course, that we cannot. God will work His character and righteousness into us by His Holy Spirit alone.

So, knowledge about God is a good thing, but knowing God personally and intimately is most important. And knowing Him is gained by quietness of heart and listening. By the power of the Spirit alone we will be transformed and share His nature as we spend time with Him in the silence.

There is an occurrence in John 12:28-29 when God spoke audibly to Jesus. Some of the people there heard thunder, some thought an angel had spoken and some understood who spoke and what He said. Here we see varying degrees of understanding of the voice of God.

Like a child grows in their understanding of a language by simply hearing it spoken, so we can grow in our understanding by being with God and listening for His voice. It may seem to us to progress so slowly as to be a waste of time, but these moments with God are never wasted. Like a great redwood tree, the growth is slow and sure, producing a deep and strong life, rooted and grounded in love.

"Father God, help me to be patient as I wait on You. Show me little signs of progress in hearing Your voice."

Week Two

The Practice of Silence

2.1

The Cleansing of Silence

"... Christ also loved the Church and gave Himself for her, that He might sanctify and cleanse her with the washing of water by the word." Eph. 5:25-26

What you fill your mind and spirit with- through conversation, television, film, music, books, magazines, the internet- will spill out of you. Jesus said "out of the abundance of the heart the mouth speaks." We are revealed by our words. It is very important that we guard our hearts and minds.

In the silence of prayer alone with God we fill our hearts with all that He is and has to give us. As we listen to Him we find ourselves purified simply by hearing Him. Paul says in Ephesians 5:26 that we are cleansed by the washing of the water of the Word. More pointedly, it says that Jesus cleanses us, we do not cleanse ourselves.

In John 15:3 Jesus says "you are already clean through the word which I have spoken to you." It is in hearing His word- a conversation, in a relationship- that the purifying occurs. We listen for His word; He cleanses us.

We may have been taught that His word is only the Bible and so that cleansing happens as we read it. The Bible is indeed the holiest of books- the treasure of God!- and reading it is a good and necessary habit to have. But many people over the centuries have read the Bible and never experienced the cleansing of God's word. Hebrews 4:12 tells us that the word of God is alive. It is this Living Word that will purify and sanctify us.

Remember the hymn we quoted earlier- "Beyond the sacred page, I seek Thee, Lord." The most effective, indeed the only life-giving way to read the Bible is in the presence of God. The Word of God (Jesus) will make the word of God (the Bible) come alive to us.

As we rest in the silence of God's presence and listen for His word we become full of His goodness, His holiness, His desires and His life. Here is another secret of the silence; We are made clean and strong through it.

This must begin, though, with confession and repentance. We must recognize our sin before God and be willing to leave it. God cannot forgive excuses. He can only forgive sin. The path to true stillness of heart and confidence before God starts with confession and repentance.

"Father, I am a sinner. All my foolish ways are known to You. Please forgive me, cleanse me and give me the strength to leave these sins behind and be like You. Keep me mindful of my constant need for You. Help me to be naked and unashamed before You."

Our quiet times with God strengthen us to resist the evil influences that surround us and to stand firm in the character of God, having the mind of Christ. In fact, because we are being conformed to His image and washed clean, we are sensitized to those things that are not of Him- dirty, compromised, superfluous or unnecessary. We see more and more clearly the way He sees.

As we listen to God He reveals Himself to us. As He reveals Himself to us He also imparts His character to us. As He imparts His character to us He also gives us His strength to stand for Him in wicked and trying circumstances; Contra Mundum- against the world- as the ancients called it.

To be contra mundum is to hate the world so fiercely that we refuse to live the same way or adopt the same principles. Yet it does not mean that we hate the people who live in the world. In fact, being with Jesus in the silence makes more clear to us how much He loves people. And as we are conformed to His image we, by this virtue, love the people of this world more as well.

We seek the delicate balance of being contra mundum without being contra populus- against the people. God helps us to love wicked people without loving what they do or joining them in it.

"Father God, give me Your character. Stamp on me the unmistakable image and love of Your son, Jesus Christ."

2.2

The Confession of Silence

"If we confess our sins, He is faithful and just to forgive us our sins and to cleanse us from all unrighteousness." 1 Jn. 1:9

It may seem odd in a book about silence to write about confession. But true silence and stillness of heart will not come to us until we have laid before Him all our foolishness and sin. The goal of confession is to be like Adam and Eve in the garden- naked and unashamed before God.

We may hide from all others our secret sins and unworthy activities, but we cannot hide them from God. All our sins are known to Him. And still He calls us to confess them openly to Him.

He does this for our good, not His. He has no need to hear our confession. It is we who need to speak openly to Him the words that reveal our souls.

> *"I acknowledged my sin to You,*
> *and my iniquity I have not hidden.*
> *I said, 'I will confess my transgressions*
> *to the Lord,'*
> *and You forgave the iniquity of my sin."*
> Ps. 32:5

> *"Now therefore, make confession to the*
> *Lord God of your fathers,*
> *and do His will."* Ezra 10:11

Confession leads to forgiveness, forgiveness to cleanliness of heart, and cleanliness of heart to confidence and joy before God. We do not seek to justify or explain our actions. We are not passing the blame to someone else. We accept the responsibility- "I have sinned"- and by that receive His forgiveness and cleansing.

Through confession of our sins we also accept God's judgment of us and His standard of righteousness. We do not judge ourselves by ourselves. We are judged by His righteousness alone, saved by His sacrifice alone, cleansed by His blood alone.

When Nathan the prophet confronted

King David about his adultery with Bathsheba, David did not reject, resent or deny his accusation. Rather, he confessed and repented. Psalm 51 is his record of this.

> *"Have mercy upon me, O God*
> *According to Your lovingkindness...*
> *And cleanse me from my sin.*
> *For I acknowledge my transgressions,*
> *And my sin is always before me..."*

David seems to also refer to this sin in Psalm 32. There he gives us a graphic image of what happens when we do not confess our sins to God.

> *When I kept silent, my bones grew old...*
> *My vitality was turned into the drought of summer."*

In other words, going without regular confessions before God causes our inner life to dry up. Like the branch that is connected to the vine, life flows into us and, in the same process, carries away our impurities. The refusal to confess stops the cleansing of our souls which, in turn, turns off the flow of His life to us.

In Psalm 51:12 David says "Restore to me the joy of Your salvation..." The joy of God comes to us as a result of confession, repentance, forgiveness and cleansing. Earlier, in verse six he says :"You desire truth in the inward parts." We often deceive ourselves about the motivations and intentions of our hearts. "The heart is deceitful above all things." (Jer. 17:9) But in the stillness and silence, raising no word of defense or explanation before Him, we allow God to expose our sin. Only then can we know it, confess it, be forgiven and free of it.

Don't be surprised then if, in the silence, you are reminded of your sins. This is a grace of God- a gift to you. It is His way of drawing you into confession, forgiveness, freedom and joy. And true stillness of heart.

"Father, as I wait before You today, give me the courage to accept Your assessment of me, to confess my sin and to be free."

2.3

The Worth of Silence

"How sweet are Your words to my taste, sweeter than honey to my mouth!" Ps. 119:103

In Luke 10 Jesus commended Mary, who sat at His feet, and rebuked Martha, who was distracted with serving and grumbling. He said to Martha "you are worried and troubled about many things. But one thing is needed and Mary has chosen that good part, which will not be taken away from her."

What good part did Mary choose but to be still and quiet at the feet of her Master?

We can, like Martha, mistake activity for fruitfulness. In fact, we can hide from God in our work for Him. We can justify going without a time of stillness in so many ways; "There is so much to do and not enough time to do it!" "I see God everyday in the faces of those I meet."

"I'm doing important work. I have no moment to spare."

Just as our bodies need sleep for restoration, so our spirits need silence and stillness. All fruitfulness and maturity will grow from this time we spend with God. Besides, the things we do could easily be done by many others. We are not indispensable to the work of God. We sometimes get an exaggerated sense of the importance of what we do.

Remember, we each will die, and the world around us will be sad for a time. But soon enough the sorrow will ebb, the wounds will heal, the laughter will return and the world will carry on without us. This is not to say you are not important to God. In fact, it is to say precisely the opposite. God loves you much more than anything you do for Him. It is your relationship with Him, not your work for Him, that He holds most dear.

Here is another secret of the silence. God is not nearly as concerned about what you do for Him as He is what time you spend with Him. You were not called to be a servant but a friend. (John 15:15) Friends know each other in deeper ways than a servant knows his master.

In John 17:3 Jesus tells us that eternity is in a relationship with the Living God. "This is eternal life, that they might know You, the only true God, and Jesus Christ whom You have sent." We are called to do more than simply obey the commands we read in the Bible. We are called to friendship and communion with God; a deep knowing, each of the other.

Here is another of the secrets of the silence; all our activity will be informed and empowered by the time we spend alone with God. Our fruitfulness will be that much greater for us having deep roots in the soil of divine friendship.

You were made first for silence, then obedience;

First for stillness, then action;

First for fellowship, then fruitfulness.

Psalm 81:13 says "O, that My people would listen to Me, that Israel would walk in My ways." Listening precedes walking. If you are to do as God says you must sit quiet and listen for Him. It is in the silence that we hear and know the will of God for us. It is here that He confirms to our hearts His plan for us.

We sometimes have the mistaken idea that God wants us to rest only after we have accomplished some task for Him, but not before. We can become so busy doing His work that we forget that He first called us to Himself. He did not say "Come to my fields." He said "Come to Me." He sent the disciples out only after they had been with Him for a time.

Before we enter the fields for the harvest we must enter the house of the Lord, find Him in the secret place and, like Mary, simply be with Him. He will send us out in His time.

Do not be in a hurry to make your way out of the presence of God. There is no greater hour spent than the hour of prayer.

"Dear Father, give me a quiet heart that I might hear You, know You and walk with You. Let the power of Your life be evident in me today."

2.4

The Dimension of Silence

"And when He opened the seventh seal, there was silence in heaven for about half an hour. And I saw the seven angels who stand before God..."
Rev. 8:1-2

Here is another secret of the silence: Silence and stillness are our doorway to the spiritual dimension, the place where God lives. As we have noted before, there is an unseen dimension to the universe that is full of life and activity. Throughout the Bible we read stories of people whose spiritual senses have been heightened enough to 'see' and 'hear' in the spirit world.

Isaiah (Is. 6) and Daniel (Dan. 7) peered into heaven. Jesus communed with Moses and Elijah on the Mount of Transfiguration. Peter saw a vision while in a trance. Paul was carried away to the third heaven. John recorded many things he saw in this dimension in the Book of the Revelation.

We will be drawn fully into this realm when we step into eternity. However, God has invited us to become acquainted with it and participate in it here and now. In John 4, Jesus told the woman at the well that God is a spirit and those who worship Him must worship in spirit and truth. To know and worship God in spirit is not an option, it is a necessity.

Some Christians have a faith based in the intellect. They study to show themselves approved of God. Others base their practice of faith in the material world. Their emphasis is on the good works Jesus told us to do. These are good and necessary to the full Christian life, but they should not be the foundation or center of our experience of God.

Rather, God is calling us into life in another dimension, the mystery of faith. He woos and teases, like the lover in Song of Solomon, that we might rise up, follow and search for Him. Proverbs 25:2 says "it is the glory of God to conceal a matter; it is the glory of kings to search out a matter." He hides; we search for Him. He is a mystical Being and ours is a mystical faith.

Some may say that it is a dangerous thing

to explore the spiritual dimension, and they are right. There is no promised land without giants to face. However, we have been given a trustworthy guide, the Holy Spirit. We do not go it alone. As we remain in Christ, yielded to the Spirit, God will protect and defend us from all evil. We can trust Him.

Do not let fear keep you from all or anything that God has for you.

What keeps us from developing the senses necessary to function in the unseen world are the various stimulations of the physical world. We learned as newborn babies to recognize shapes and sound, and understand distance and perspective. We crawled and stood and walked. We listened and learned the voices of our parents. We learned to use our five physical senses.

Just so we must begin again as babes to grow in the senses of the spiritual world. We learn to 'see' and 'hear' with our hearts. We listen and recognize the voice of God. We grow to understand what He is saying to us, just like when we were children.

To grow in the spirit it is helpful, even necessary, to eliminate as much of the outward, physical stimulation as we can. This allows us without distraction to focus our attention on God Himself.

Our eyes will not help us here. Our ears will not help us here. Silence and stillness become the medium through which we develop our spiritual senses.

Jesus often went at night into the desert to pray. He encouraged us to go into the closet of prayer. These are both strong images of a place where our outward senses are deprived of stimuli. Likewise, David sought God in the cleft of the rock. Elijah met Him in a cave. Moses went to the mountain alone. All solitary. All removed from human contact and conversation.

It is important that we find a place of solitude where we can turn our attention away from the cares of this world and toward the things of God. David calls it the secret place. We should think of it in this way, too. It is a place where we know we will not be disturbed; where there will be no demand on our time or attention.

"Father, give me the courage to seek you in the mystery of faith. I commit my ways to You and trust that the Holy Spirit will guide and protect me."

2.5

The Enemies of Silence

"Catch us the foxes, the little foxes that spoil the vines, for our vines have tender grapes.."
Song of Songs. 2:15

The enemies of silence are many- the urgent and the mundane, the serious and the frivolous, both weighty and trivial responsibilities, and, especially, the enemy of your very soul.

As we mentioned before, the spiritual world is full of life and activity, not all of it on your side. There are those beings whose desire is to steal, kill and destroy you. They will use every means at their disposal to keep you from the silence. They know the power that awaits you if they do not stop you.

Most of the time, however, the distractions that keep us from prayer won't appear to be a concerted spiritual attack on us by a dedicated demonic army. It will often seem simply that the necessities of life are crowding us, calling us away from the silence with God.

Song of Solomon 2:15 says to "catch us the foxes, the little foxes that spoil the vines..." It is so often the trivial, frivolous and mundane- the little foxes- that spoil our intentions to be alone with God. The lion and the bear are easy to recognize as enemies. It's the little things that easily escape our notice that will keep us from this very important calling.

It is in the discipline of prayer that we learn the difference between the things we *should* do and the things we *must* do. When we do without our time with God each day and move directly into the responsibilities that call so urgently to us we forego the opportunity to learn to judge the true worth of every activity and put it in its proper perspective and place in our lives.

Solomon goes on in this verse to say that "our vines have tender grapes." In this twenty one day journey into silent prayer we are at the very beginning of our fruit-bearing. We have not yet seen the mature fruit of silence and solitude with God. We may think that the small amount of fruit- the tender grapes- we see presently is not much of a loss should the little foxes get them.

Zechariah 4:10 asks "Who has despised the day of small things?" Jesus said in Mark 4:30-32 that the mustard seed, though small, would grow to be great. If we look down upon our small beginnings we will never experience the fruitfulness God has for us. These tender grapes, when protected and nourished, will bear fruit in their season.

This time alone with God must be considered inviolable. It is not a *should*; it is a *must*. Though the fruit may seem so small and the growth so slow, yet it will grow to be protection and provision for us in God's time.

In the silence before God we learn to recognize the enemies of God and our own souls. We easily see the lion and the bear. Everyone sees them. But God desires to give us discernment to see the little foxes, the silent predators, the small diversions and urgencies that are more easily used by our enemy to keep us from bearing fruit in the Spirit.

Paul prayed for the Ephesian church (1:18) that the eyes of their hearts would be enlightened. That is our prayer today. We ask God to open our eyes to see clearly the little foxes- even the very smallest- that would keep us from being with Him.

James said (1:5) that if we lacked wisdom, we should ask God for it and He would give it to us without reproach. As we are with God in this receptive silence He will uncover our enemies.

Paul tells us in Ephesians 6:10-18 to put on the whole armor of God. It would be good to read that section of scripture now. In it Paul shows us how we can triumphantly resist our enemy.

"Dear Jesus, help me to avoid distractions and resist the enemies of my soul as I come to You today. Give me discernment in Your Spirit."

2.6

The Solitude of Silence

"...the gospel which was preached by me is not according to man. For I neither received it nor was I taught it, but it came through the revelation of Jesus Christ." Gal. 1:11-12

Humans tend to be gregarious beings. We band together for common purposes in clubs, fraternities, organizations, churches and nations. We do the things we do in community.

However, the silence we are called to is found not in community but in solitude. We may be tempted to form a little circle of like-minded Christians to practice the silence together, but that is not what God is calling you to. This is a fundamental secret of the silence; it is practiced alone.

People innately know that this is the case. Every religion in every part of the world esteems the ascetic who has gone into the lonely places in search of something divine or transcendent. The Christian withdraws into silence and solitude so that he may find Christ.

The Gospels tell us over and over of Jesus retreating to the mountains or desert alone. After Jesus was baptized by John in the Jordan river he went into the desert for forty days of prayer. He was alone with the Father. Even on the night He was betrayed He took His disciples with Him to the garden but then went a distance away from them to pray alone.

If Jesus sought solitude in prayer should we expect to do any different?

Paul was alone for three years after his life changing experience on the road to Damascus. He says that what he received in this time he received from Christ alone. In Galatians 1:16 he says "I did not immediately confer with flesh and blood."

If Paul was in no hurry to confer with other people, should we be?

We all came into the world alone and will so depart from it. We will stand before God alone on the day of judgment. It is true that we are called to care for one another in the community of faith, but we cannot answer for each other before God. He calls us to Himself alone.

Many believers have been taught that it is dangerous to learn of God apart from the Church. They are right, and I am not suggesting that you spend all your life in the solitude. We have been given to each other to sharpen, correct, comfort, encourage and provoke one another to godliness.

However, this fearful reasoning can become a convenient excuse for living without the silence and solitude of prayer entirely. Let me state it plainly; your relationship with Jesus Christ does not begin or have its foundation in the community of believers. You are called first to Him alone.

Jesus did not call His followers to "join the team" or "come to the services." He didn't even call them to His teaching. He said, and still says, "come to Me." It is an amazing, profound, terrifying and awesome privilege and responsibility He has extended to His followers.

Jesus calls you to Himself.

The word of the Lord was given to the

prophets in solitude and silence. In fact, Jeremiah says in Lamentations 3:25-28

> *"The Lord is good to those who wait for Him,*
> *To the soul who seeks Him.*
> *It is good that one should hope*
> *And wait quietly for the salvation of the Lord...*
> *Let him sit alone and be silent,*
> *Because God has laid it upon him..."*

"Jesus, teach me to seek You alone and to find in You alone the fountain of truth."

2.7

Abiding in Silence

"Abide in Me, and I in you. As the branch cannot bear fruit of itself, unless it abides in the vine, neither can you unless you abide in Me."
John 15:4

On the night Jesus was betrayed He spoke very movingly to His disciples. He talked of His great love for them and the work of the Holy Spirit in them, and He prayed for them.

One theme He spoke about at length was that of abiding in Him, like a branch abides in a vine. The imagery is deep and powerful and deserves our contemplation. The context- that His departure and death were imminent- gives these words greater importance.

The word for abide used in the Greek is *meno*. It speaks of a state of being and a sense of stillness and rest. It means to stay or remain. The idea is that this is a continuing, permanent state, not an off and on recurring one.

This is borne out by the agrarian metaphor that Jesus used. Branches do not visit vines when they need sustenance. They do not come and go. They stay. They are attached. If they detach, they die.

Jesus is telling us that we are to constantly be with Him, in Him. We do not come and go. We remain. This is the only way we receive the life of the Spirit. Just like the vine, the life flows to us simply because we are attached and stay- abide- in Him.

The branch doesn't have to plead for the nutrients it needs to grow. It only needs to abide in the vine. There is no necessary activity. Simply remaining is all that is needed.

So Jesus calls us to stay, remain, abide in Him. He calls us to the place of rest that is abiding. As we remain in Him the life flows to us. Everything we need from God for holiness and godly living comes to us when we abide.

In these times when people change careers, homes, cars, styles, spouses and interests without much thought or regret it seems quaint, even anachronistic, to introduce the idea of staying with something an entire lifetime. Yet that is what the follower of Jesus is called to do.

Stay. Remain. Abide.

Jesus tells us plainly that we cannot bear fruit without abiding. We may engage in Christian activities and worthy spiritual pursuits, but our fruitfulness is entirely dependent on our abiding in Him.

What fruit is He speaking of? It is not to do with those things that people may count as important- influence, prestige or acclaim- nor is it the result of anything we may do for Him. It is the fruit of the Spirit- love, joy, peace, patience, gentleness, goodness, faith, meekness and temperance. Gal.5:22

The fruit mentioned here are not accomplishments but character traits. These are not what we do but who we are- the foundation of our person. Jesus is more concerned with who you are than any activity or accomplishment you may undertake or enjoy. It is vital that we understand this. The benefits of prayer are not counted in accomplishments but in character.

Again, Jesus is more concerned with who

you are than what you do. He measures you by the shape of your character, and His traits can only be had by abiding in Him like the branch to the vine.

I have known many Christians who somehow lost touch with this necessity. They seemed to feel that they had outgrown abiding in the vine. Perhaps they hoped to encounter Jesus incidentally on their way to other things. This kind of thinking is a trap that will sap your spiritual life just like a branch separated from the vine withers and dies.

It cannot be made any more plain. Our fruitfulness is entirely dependent on our being connected to Jesus and abiding in Him. No Christian matures out of this need. In fact, the greater the mantle of responsibility we have in the family of God, the greater the need to abide, spend time with Jesus in the silence and let our spirits be strengthened.

"Jesus, You are the vine and I am Your branch. Help me to abide in You every moment of every hour of every day of my whole life."

Week Three

The Way of Silence

3.1

Voices in Silence

"There are, it may be, so many voices in the world, and none of them is without signification." 1 Cor. 14:10

There are indeed many voices in the world clamoring for our attention. Each of them is giving us a way to think about God and ourselves. Some incite us to anger, envy, lust, love or some other similar passion, while others tell us how to behave or what we need and don't have.

Some of the voices we hear tell us about God and what He thinks about us. We may have been brought up to believe that God is like Santa Claus- making a list, checking it twice and finding out who's naughty or nice. Alternately, we may believe that God is benevolent but aloof, preferring to remain distant from his little human creations.

Some voices in our lives tell us about our failures, remind us of our past sins and reinforce a negative self identity. If we believe these voices, we will think of ourselves as worthless, ineffective, unloved and not fit for friendship with God.

Still others encourage in us a sense of pride and entitlement; that we should have what we want because we have a right to have it; that our concerns and desires are most important and should be served. This can make us think that either we don't need God or that He should be our butler, attending to our wishes and giving us what we want.

The voice with the most powerful impact on us is our own. What we say to ourselves- about ourselves and God- will determine what we believe and, consequently, how we live. It will form the framework of our theology- our knowledge of God- and our understanding of ourselves.

Can we expect to know the mind of God if we never listen to Him? If we only listen to our own counsel we'll only believe what we know about ourselves. It is when we listen to God that we hear what He knows about us.

As we have mentioned before, silence is a necessary part of conversation. In the conversation of prayer, the silence is our time to listen for Jesus and know Him; what is most important to Him, how He thinks about us and His world. I am of the opinion that this aspect of silent prayer is the most powerful antidote to false and worldly thinking.

We know from the Bible many of God's attitudes toward us.

> *"Blessed be the God and Father of our Lord Jesus Christ, who has blessed us with every spiritual blessing in the heavenly places in Christ..."* Eph. 1:3

> *"There is therefore now no condemnation to those who are in Christ Jesus..."* Rom. 8:1

> *"In this is love, not that we loved God, but that He loved us..."* 1 Jn. 4:10

> *"For God did not send His Son into the world to condemn the world but that the world through Him might be saved."* John 3:17

> *"But God, who is rich in mercy, because of His great love with which He loved us..."* Eph. 2:4

When we read these Scriptures in the presence of God, He confirms them to us in a way mere printed words cannot. His Spirit calls to our own spirits so that our understanding might be changed and, as Paul said, we can "have the mind of Christ." (1 Cor. 2:16)

To have the mind of Christ is to think His thoughts, agree with His perspective, believe Him, trust that He loves us and repeat to ourselves His words in our own voice- our agreement with and acceptance of God's word. This will do more to mitigate the influence of false thinking than anything else you can do.

"Let this mind be in you which was also in Christ Jesus..." Phil. 2:5

This secret of the silence is that our mind is changed and renewed as we listen to His voice. God, who is most wise and most loving, desires that we should believe Him above all others.

"Father God, all wise, all powerful, all loving, speak to me today and give me the mind of Christ."

3.2

Stillness in Silence

"Meditate within your heart on your bed, and be still." Ps. 4:4

"Be still, and know that I am God. I will be exalted among the nations, I will be exalted in the earth!" Ps. 46:10

The stillness we seek in the silence is more than an absence of physical motion. It is a stillness of heart and mind and emotion. Even more, it is the submission of our will to the will of God.

How must the warriors of Israel have strained at the command to stand still and let God win the victory! They who were trained to fight stood at the ready on the field of battle and yet were commanded not to move.

How puzzled the disciples must have

been as the high priest and his men came to arrest Jesus in the garden of Gethsemane when, wanting to act in defense of their Master, were instead told by Jesus to "permit even this."

We find ourselves in similar circumstances, when the course of action that could result in our victory seems clear to us, and yet God commands us to be still. Our logic tells us that we must act. Our God tells us we must not. It is very much like a dog whose owner has thrown a stick and said "Stay!"

As we have said before, if we will fight our battles, God will not. If we insist on acting when told to be still, God will allow us to work to the end of our resources. If we will see the power of God to gain the victory we must allow Him to act on our behalf.

We must be still.

The stillness we learn in the silence is training us to obey the voice of God in all of our circumstances. There is a saying that a biddable dog is a good dog. One which does the bidding of his master is the one that can be trusted.

God calls us to quiet our hearts in His presence that we may know and recognize that still center of the spinning world in our everyday lives. If we know it in prayer we will see it when God calls us to it in trying times.

This is the only way we free God to win the victory for us.

> *"And Moses said to the people, 'Do not be afraid. Stand still, and see the salvation of the Lord, which He will accomplish for you today."* Ex 14:13

Moses did not say these words in leisurely circumstances. He was leading an argumentative, slave-minded band of Israelites out of Egypt. Behind them stood the most powerful army in all the world. Before them rolled the waves of the Red Sea. To the Israelites death seemed imminent and sure. Resistance was futile, and standing still was much less preferable to running away.

And yet God commanded them to do just that. Why? So they could see His salvation. Perhaps Moses learned this secret during his forty years on the backside of the desert. God's action, in times like these, seems to be in inverse proportion to ours.

If we will be still, He will act. He will be strong for the weak. He will defend the defenseless. He will speak up for those who have no voice. He will act on behalf of those who will be still.

When the Israelites obeyed and stood still, God opened a way for them where there was no way. God, who does not change, still does that today for those who will obey His voice.

The stillness of heart, submission to His will and obedience to His voice that we learn in the silence will prepare us for the times when we hear Him call to us as He did to them in the desert; "Be still, and see the salvation of the Lord."

"Father, teach me to trust You and to be still when You command it of me."

3.3

The Holy Silence

"Hear, O Israel; The Lord our God, the Lord is one!." Deut.. 6:4

You may ask "if God speaks to me, what will He say?" No one can answer that exactly, but there is one thing we can safely expect.

God will always speak to us in accordance with the Bible. The reason for this is simple; the God who gave us the Holy Scriptures is the same God that speaks to you today. He has not changed.

The Bible speaks of God being holy. This means more than that He is without sin. To be holy is to be full and complete in oneself, lacking nothing. Because God is full and complete in Himself, lacking nothing, there is no change that can make Him more full or more complete. Therefore, any change would be to diminish who

He is. So, God never changes.

> *"Jesus Christ the same yesterday, today and forever."* Hebrews 13:8

> *"For I am the Lord, I do not change..."* Malachi 3:6

Because He never changes, all that He says or does will be consistent with who He is and with what He has said or done in the past. There is an essential harmony to everything about God- His character, acts and words.

Deuteronomy 6:4 says of God that He is one. This tells us that there is a fundamental unity to His being. Every thing He says and everything He does will bear the stamp of His character. He never acts "out of character."

For this reason, all that God says to you in the silence can be confirmed in the Bible. Some may come to the silence expecting a new revelation. Ecclesiastes 1:9 tells us plainly that there is nothing new under the sun.

If we find that what we believe we are hearing from God in prayer is not consistent with His character or the Bible, we should surely submit it to godly counsel for confirmation. We should not be so arrogant as to think that God will speak to us alone some special truth He would not say to any other. The secrets of the silence are not occult or hidden. The silence of prayer is practiced in the full light of God.

What God reveals to you in the silence can, with diligent searching, be found echoed and confirmed in the Bible. In fact, searching the Scriptures will unfold a deeper understanding of what God has spoken to you.

Finding the echo of God's voice in the Bible will also give you confidence that you are hearing Him truly. It is the earthly touchstone for all that we receive in the silence.

What we hear from God in prayer will never be "out of tune" with the rest of His song or contradict His character as shown in the Bible. He is One. He is holy. He is the same yesterday, today and forever.

We may also hear the same word God speaks to us being echoed in our daily lives- in casual conversation or other ways. It can seem at times that the whole universe is calling to us and repeating the word of God to us.

In other readings and in sermons and

teachings we may also hear His voice. These are all God's way of confirming His word to you and building your confidence in your ability to hear from Him.

"God, who at various times and in various ways spoke in time past to the fathers by the prophets, has in these last days spoken to us by His Son, whom He has appointed heir of all things, through whom also he made the worlds." Hebrews 1:1-2

"Father, confirm Your word to me in the Bible, through godly counsel and in every experience I have today."

3.4

The Names of God

"...And in His law he meditates day and night." Ps. 1:2

Throughout the Bible we are told to meditate. Our meditation is, however, not unfocused. We are told continually to meditate "on" something- His word, laws, judgments, names, Himself.

Whereas other religions practice an emptiness of mind or spirit in their meditation, we are called to have a mental or spiritual object on which we meditate, centered on God Himself.

"This Book of the Law shall not depart from your mouth, but you shall meditate in it day and night." Joshua 1:8

"I meditate on You in the night watches." Ps. 63:6

"My meditation of Him shall be sweet."
Ps. 104:34

"The name of the Lord is a strong tower; the righteous run to it and are safe." Prov. 18:10

One helpful habit we may embrace is the reading of a section of the Bible each day. There are 31 Proverbs, one for each day of the longest months. There are 150 Psalms, five for each of 30 days. We may read one of Paul's epistles and meditate on it.

We may find on some days that one verse fills our hearts and we have not enough time to plumb its depths. As we meditate on His words we are always seeking to find Him there.

Another habit we may develop is to choose one of the names of God each day and ponder it, meditate on it, think deeply about it in the silence of prayer. In the Bible names are not merely signifiers of specific people. They tell us something about the person. Likewise, each name by which God is known reveals to us an aspect of His character.

God our maker (Ps. 95:6)

Lion of the tribe of Judah (Rev. 5:5)

Wonderful, Counselor, Mighty God, Prince of Peace (Isaiah 9:6)

Lamb of God (John 1:29)

God our righteousness (Jer. 23:6)

God our miracle (Ex. 17:15)

God our healer (Ex. 15:26)

Emmanuel- God With Us (Is. 7:14)

Author and Finisher of our faith (Heb. 12:2)

The Way, the Truth and the Life (John 14:6)

God our Redeemer (Ps; 19:14)

Consuming Fire (Deut. 4:24)

God our refuge (Ps. 90:1)

Shepherd (Ps. 23:1)

I Am That I Am (Ex. 3:14)

The Lord who sees (Gen. 22:14)

There are spiritual riches to be discovered in meditating on His names. We can know more fully who Jesus is and how He works through the thoughtful, prayerful consideration of the names of God.

"Jesus, reveal Yourself to me as I meditate on Your name."

3.5

Words and Silence

"In the multitude of words sin is not lacking, but he who restrains his lips is wise." Pr. 10:19

"A fool also is full of words..." Ec. 10:14

"A fool's mouth is his destruction, and his lips are the snare of his soul." Pr. 18:7

"A fool vents all his feelings, but a wise man holds them back." Pr. 29:11

"He who has knowledge spares his words, and a man of understanding is of a calm spirit." Pr. 17:27

"Let the words of my mouth and the meditation of my heart be acceptable in Your sight, O Lord, my strength and my Redeemer." Ps. 19:14

"Do not be hasty with your mouth, and let not your heart utter anything hastily before God. For God is in His heaven, and you are on earth; therefore let your words be few." Ec. 5:2

Words have power. We may consider many thoughts and opinions in our hearts, but once we say them aloud the very act of speaking them will somehow solidify them into something we believe to be true.

Our thoughts on anything are, by virtue of our limitations of knowledge and information, subjective and incomplete. God, on the other hand, has all information and knowledge and, therefore, has the wisest thoughts and best perspective on everything.

If we believe that God is right about everything, we will prefer to believe as He believes and doubt all others, including ourselves. When we are hasty to speak before Him, we not only forego the wisest counsel in the universe, we also strengthen our belief in our own opinion.

The Bible is very clear that many words are the province of the fool. The wise person chooses words carefully and speaks less, even in prayer. It goes even further to suggest that many words produce sin. Can we be wise without learning to hold our tongues?

Hasty words are often bitter, angry, sometimes insolent words. The words we most regret and wish we could recall are the ones spoken without thought.

God calls us to speak less and develop a calm spirit in the silence of prayer. There is the first obvious benefit that we hear from the all wise God, who is the Living Word and greatly desires to communicate with us, and learn to live beyond our own counsel.

The second benefit is that what we learn in the silence of prayer helps us hold our tongues in everyday conversations. What we practice alone with God we also extend to the rest of our lives and relationships.

Like Peter on the Mount of Transfiguration we sometimes speak when we don't really have anything to say. Perhaps we speak out of nervous energy. Or perhaps we have an exalted opinion of ourselves, believing that everyone must have the benefit of our insight.

Years ago I had vocal nodules and was forbidden to speak by the doctor for six weeks. In our weekly gatherings with a small group of fellow Christians I was accustomed to sharing what I thought were unique insights. Besides the frustration of not being part of the discussion, I was humbled to find that everything that I thought to say was eventually said by someone else, often with greater clarity.

God desires us to be wise, not foolish. He calls us to the discipline of silence to gain mastery over our tongues. Like Peter, God calls us to hear Him.

"Father God, teach me to hold my tongue, consider my words and be wise."

3.6

Pneuma

"It shall come to pass that before they call, I will answer; and while they are still speaking, I will hear." Is. 65:24

"... and upholding all things by the word of His power..." Heb. 1:3

"Before I formed you in the womb I knew you..." Jer. 1:5

"For from Him and through Him and to Him are all things, to whom be glory forever. Amen." Rom. 11:36

"I am the Way, and the Truth, and the Life." Jn. 14:6

We sometimes make the mistake of believing that we are walking on God's way, as though it was something He set out for us apart from Himself. Jesus tells us not that He is the maker of the way, but that He *is* the way. He doesn't tell us truth; He *is* Truth. He doesn't give us life; He *is* Life. He is the Pneuma.

For some this may be a subtle and unnecessary distinction. But to understand Pneuma praying, we must know that God is closer to us than our very breath. In truth, He is our very breath. He is the Pneuma.

God our Father promises that He will answer before we call to Him. That can only be possible if He is hearing something other than our voices. It can only be that He is listening in on the silent cry of our hearts. Before He formed us, He knew us, and knows us still.

Why then, do we even pray out loud? It certainly doesn't enable God to hear us better. The benefits of spoken prayer are for us, both personally and in the communion of the Church. It helps us that we verbally acknowledge our dependence on God, and cast all our cares on Him.

But to be Peniel, face to face with God, is to need nothing else but the Pneuma. Words are an intrusion on the relationship. We breathe out our prayers and praises; we breathe in His presence.

We are not offering requests, we are offering ourselves. We are surrendering completely everything we have and are to Him. In a delicate way it is like the love between a man and a woman.

Pneuma praying is so personal, so intimate, so unashamed and close to the heart of who we really are- and so like romance- that it is reserved for the private place of prayer, where we close the door on the rest of the world and rejoice in the love of our God. This is the knowing that Jesus refers to in John 17:3.

Pneuma prayer is not silent because it has nothing to say but because it has everything to say, and because to say anything is unnecessary. Like Paul, I speak of a mystery concerning Christ and the church. (Eph. 5:32)

I want to say again that this kind of praying is not meant to supplant or replace our verbal prayers, but to enhance and enrich them.

> *"And when you pray, do not use vain repetitions as the heathen do. For they think that they will be heard for their many words. Therefore do not be like them. For your Father knows the things*

you have need of before you ask Him."
Mt. 6:7-8

Jesus pointed out that the birds don't sow, reap or store away food in barns and the flowers don't clothe themselves and yet are dressed more splendidly than Solomon. He says to us that our heavenly Father will care for us like that. Are you not worth more than the sparrows?

"But seek first the kingdom of God and His righteousness, and all these things will be added unto you." Mt. 6:33

"Father, draw me close to You and let us be together, apart from the rest of the world."

3.7

Liturgy of Silence

*"Our Father, who art in heaven,
Hallowed be Thy name.
Thy kingdom come, Thy will be done
On earth as it is in heaven.
Give us this day our daily bread,
And forgive us our debts
as we forgive our debtors.
And lead us not into temptation,
But deliver us from evil,
For Thine is the kingdom, and the power,
And the glory forever. Amen."*
Mt. 6:9-13

Jesus told us to pray like this.

Our Father... we start with a recognition that our relationship to God is as children to their Father, not slaves to a master, subjects to a king or workers to an employer.

Hallowed be Thy name... we continue in reverent worship.

Thy kingdom come, Thy will be done on earth as it is in heaven... we voice a specific request that the rule of God should extend to all the earth.

Give us this day our daily bread... we ask for our basic needs to be met.

And forgive us our debts as we forgive our debtors... then we confess our sinfulness and ask for the same mercy that we give to others.

And lead us not into temptation, but deliver us from evil... we admit that we have a propensity to wickedness and ask for protection from an enemy that is willing to lead us into it.

For Thine is the kingdom, and the power, and the glory forever. Amen... we close with worship and a recognition that everything is His.

This is a good template for our times in the silence with God. We worship, we confess, we repent, we humble ourselves, we recognize the worth of our fellow man, we surrender all to Jesus.

Pneuma praying and meeting God in the silence is not meant to overtake our lives but to undergird them. This time with God prepares us to be like Jesus in all the daily tasks we do, the conversations we have, the thoughts we allow to occupy our minds and the acts we commit.

We begin the day with an open hand, releasing our grasp on all we possess, all rights we may think we have a claim to, our time, our very lives. We continue through the day with an open hand, refusing to hold tightly to anything, knowing that to do so could draw us away from Him. This is the surrendered life.

> *"Let this mind be in you which was also in Christ, who did not consider equality with God something to be grasped. but made Himself of no reputation, taking the form of a bondservant, and coming in the likeness of men."* Phil. 2:5-7

The final secret of the silence is that it sets us free from protecting our own status and position in the world. Is our reputation to be defended? Is our position to be protected? Will not God act on our behalf if we will stand still and see His salvation?

PrayerCanvas
for your times alone with God

Available now:
one hour of ambient prayer music (with sound of rain)

Reign

coming soon:
Deep (ocean) Glow (fire)
Soar (wind) Pulse (bass & drums)

Email info@prayercanvas.com
for new book & music releases.

---

give

hope

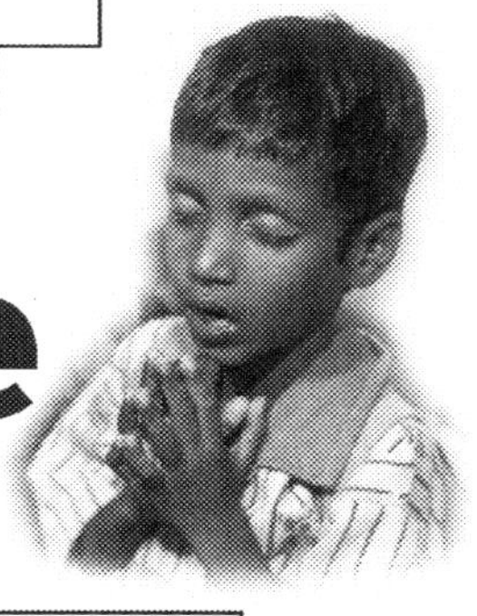

to a needy child

sponsor a child online at **www.compassion.com**

My Prayer List

Secrets of the Silence Afterword

At the beginning of the book I invited you to take the unusual challenge of writing your prayer requests out and setting them aside for the twenty one days that we would search the silence of God. Today let's revisit that list.

Has anything changed? Has God been at work on your list while you have been listening? I am confident that He has.

Here is the more important question; Have you changed? My prayer for you is that through this journey into the silence you have experienced the love, cleansing and presence of God in a new way, and that you have learned to hear and recognize His voice. I trust that you have found the simple, restful joy of being with Jesus. And I hope you are ruined for anything else!

Please tell me about your experiences through this prayer journey. I am eager to share them with others who are walking the same path. E-mail bob@prayercanvas.com.

Peniel,
Bob Kilpatrick

There is no person or power that can change our position before God. There is no authority, whether in heaven or earth, that can separate us from the love of God. All we have we have received from His hand. If He should take it away, blessed be the name of our God. We are free!

"Father, I am secure in You. Let my life be a true reflection of Your character."